HAL•LEONARD BASS PLAY-ALONG

VOL. 44

Cover photo courtesy of Capitol Records

ISBN 978-1-4584-2362-7

HAL•LEONARD®
CORPORATION

7777 W. BLUEMOUND RD. P.O. BOX 13819 MILWAUKEE, WI 53213

In Australia Contact:
Hal Leonard Australia Pty. Ltd.
4 Lentara Court
Cheltenham, Victoria, 3192 Australia
Email: ausadmin@halleonard.com.au

Visit Hal Leonard Online at
www.halleonard.com

Bass Notation Legend

Bass music can be notated two different ways: on a *musical staff*, and in *tablature*

Notes:

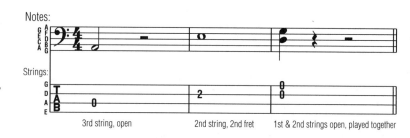

THE MUSICAL STAFF shows pitches and rhythms and is divided by bar lines into measures. Pitches are named after the first seven letters of the alphabet.

TABLATURE graphically represents the bass fingerboard. Each horizontal line represents a string, and each number represents a fret.

3rd string, open   2nd string, 2nd fret   1st & 2nd strings open, played together

HAMMER-ON: Strike the first (lower) note with one finger, then sound the higher note (on the same string) with another finger by fretting it without picking.

PULL-OFF: Place both fingers on the notes to be sounded. Strike the first note and without picking, pull the finger off to sound the second (lower) note.

LEGATO SLIDE: Strike the first note and then slide the same fret-hand finger up or down to the second note. The second note is not struck.

SHIFT SLIDE: Same as legato slide, except the second note is struck.

TRILL: Very rapidly alternate between the notes indicated by continuously hammering on and pulling off.

TREMOLO PICKING: The note is picked as rapidly and continuously as possible.

VIBRATO: The string is vibrated by rapidly bending and releasing the note with the fretting hand.

SHAKE: Using one finger, rapidly alternate between two notes on one string by sliding either a half-step above or below.

NATURAL HARMONIC: Strike the note while the fret hand lightly touches the string directly over the fret indicated.

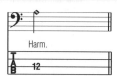

MUFFLED STRINGS: A percussive sound is produced by laying the fret hand across the string(s) without depressing them and striking them with the pick hand.

BEND: Strike the note and bend up the interval shown.

BEND AND RELEASE: Strike the note and bend up as indicated, then release back to the original note. Only the first note is struck.

RIGHT-HAND TAP: Hammer ("tap") the fret indicated with the "pick-hand" index or middle finger and pull off to the note fretted by the fret hand.

LEFT-HAND TAP: Hammer ("tap") the fret indicated with the "fret-hand" index or middle finger.

SLAP: Strike ("slap") string with right-hand thumb.

POP: Snap ("pop") string with right-hand index or middle finger.

Additional Musical Definitions

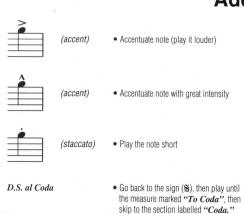

(accent)	• Accentuate note (play it louder)
(accent)	• Accentuate note with great intensity
(staccato)	• Play the note short
D.S. al Coda	• Go back to the sign (%), then play until the measure marked ***"To Coda"***, then skip to the section labelled ***"Coda."***

Fill

• Label used to identify a brief pattern which is to be inserted into the arrangement.

• Repeat measures between signs.

• When a repeated section has different endings, play the first ending only the first time and the second ending only the second time.

CONTENTS

Hangar 18

Words and Music by Dave Mustaine

5-string bass, tuning:
(low to high) D-E-A-D-G

Intro
Moderately fast ♩ = 160

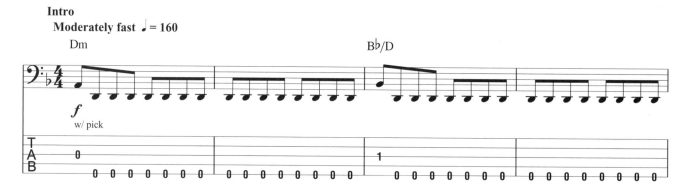

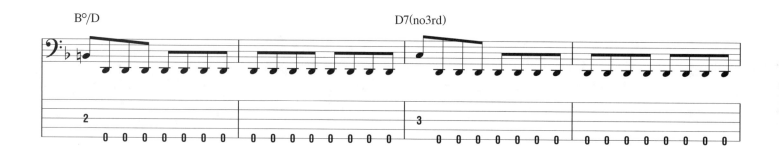

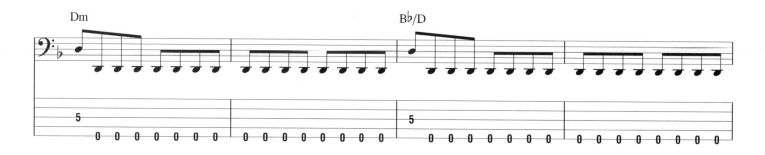

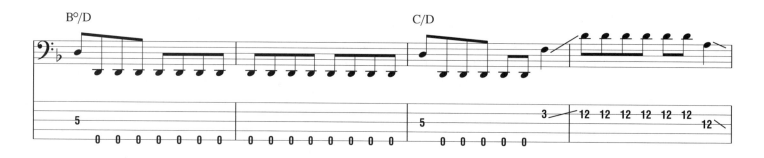

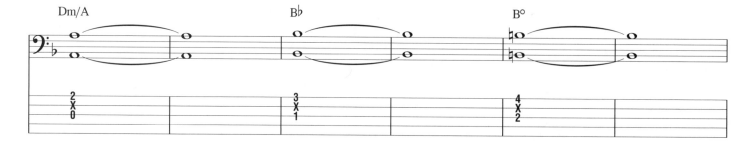

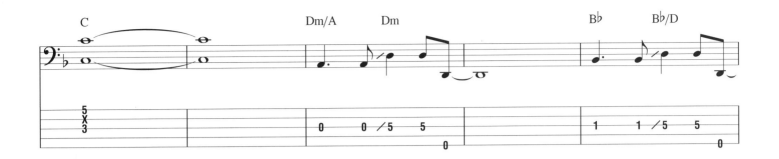

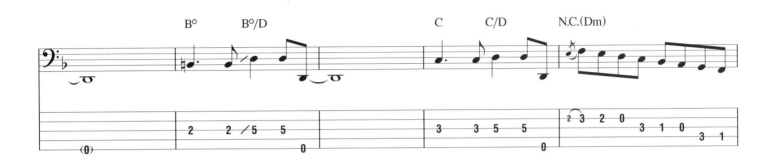

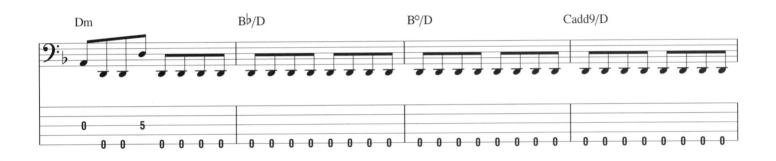

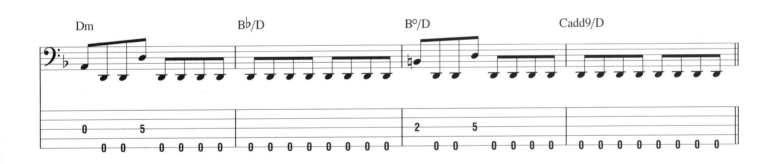

% **Verse**

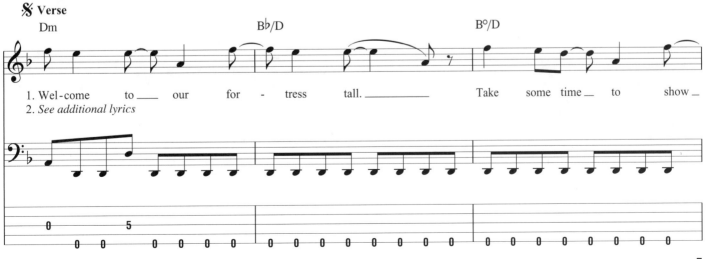

1. Wel-come   to ___ our   for - tress   tall. _____   Take   some   time__ to   show __
2. *See additional lyrics*

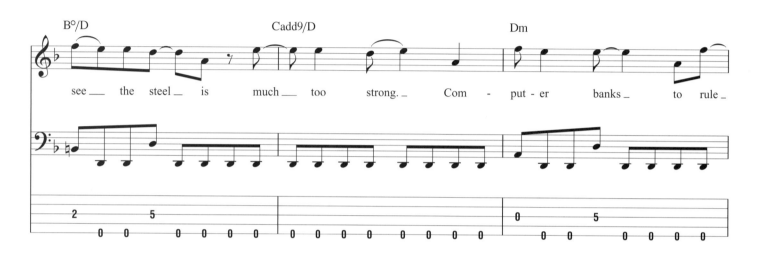

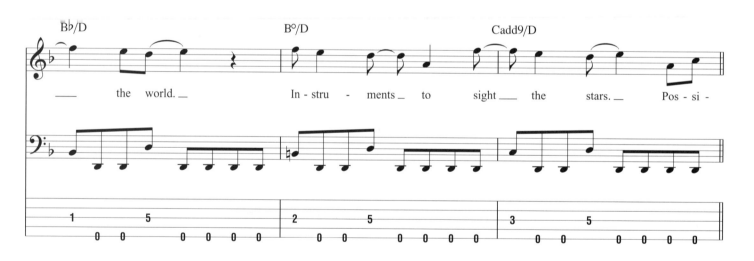

Chorus

6

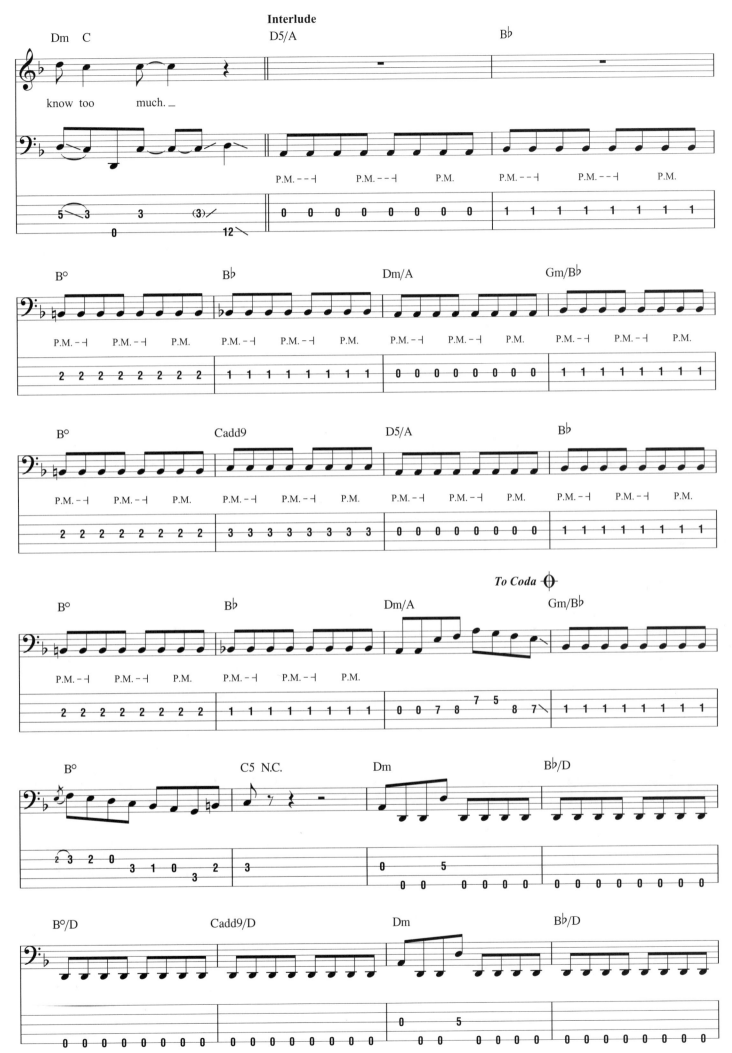

Interlude

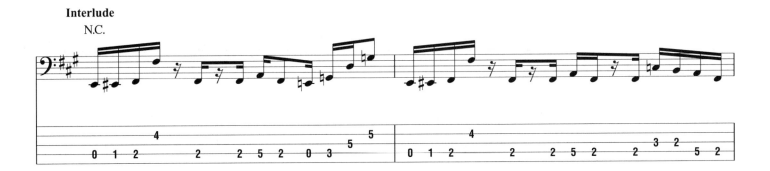

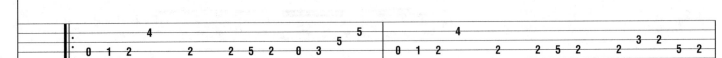

Guitar Solo
*Slightly faster ♩ = 124

*4th time, Slightly faster ♩ = 130.

Interlude

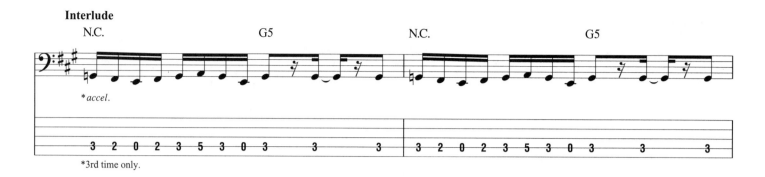

*accel.

*3rd time only.

Play 4 times

Guitar Solo

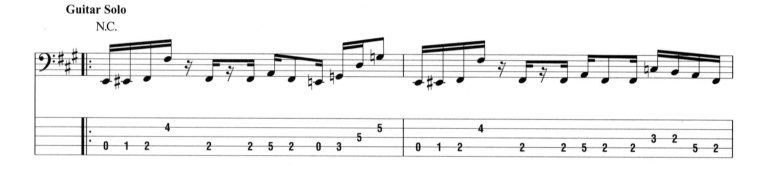

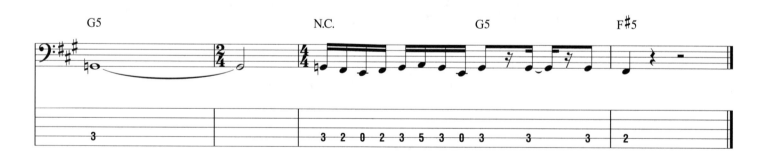

Additional Lyrics

2. Foreign life forms inventory.
Suspended state of cryogenics.
Selective amnesia's the story.
Believed foretold but who'd suspect...
The military intelligence?
Two words combined that can't make sense.

Symphony of Destruction

Words and Music by Dave Mustaine

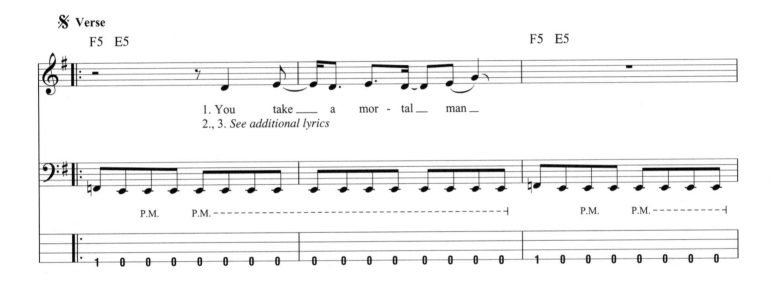

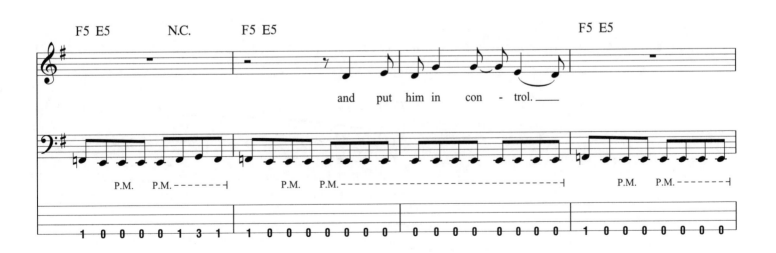

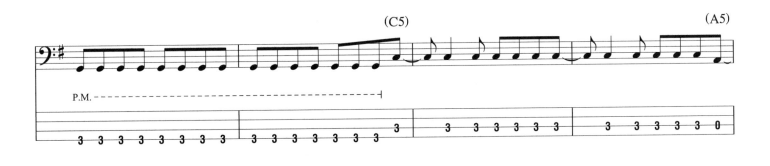

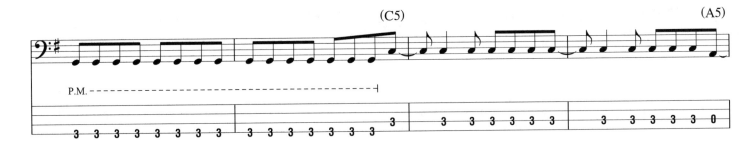

D.S. al Coda
(take 2nd ending)

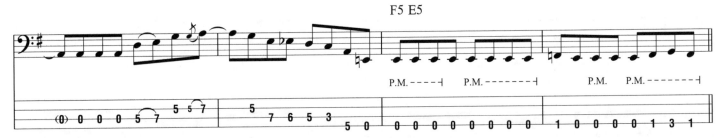

Sym - pho - ny   of ___ De - struc - tion. ___

Additional Lyrics

2. Mm, actin' like a robot,
   Its metal brain corrodes.
   You try to take its pulse
   Before the head explodes, explodes, explodes.

3. The earth starts to rumble.
   World powers fall.
   A, warring for the heavens,
   A peaceful man stands tall, a, tall, a, tall.

Head Crusher

Words and Music by Dave Mustaine and Shawn Drover

N.C.(F#5)
A5 B5 C5
be - fore its mor - ti - fi - ca - tion.
G5 F#5 E5 C5 B5 A5 G#5
Now let the tor - ture be - gin!
End double-time feel
2nd time, substitute Fill 1
A5
B5
G5
Chorus
N.C.
Death by the head crush - er.
Fill 1

Place your chin for-ward in-to the re-straint.

Your head slow-ly caves in from the com-pres-sion.

You'll faint to the black - out from ___

___ the in - fer - nal pain. _____

Ah! _____

Interlude

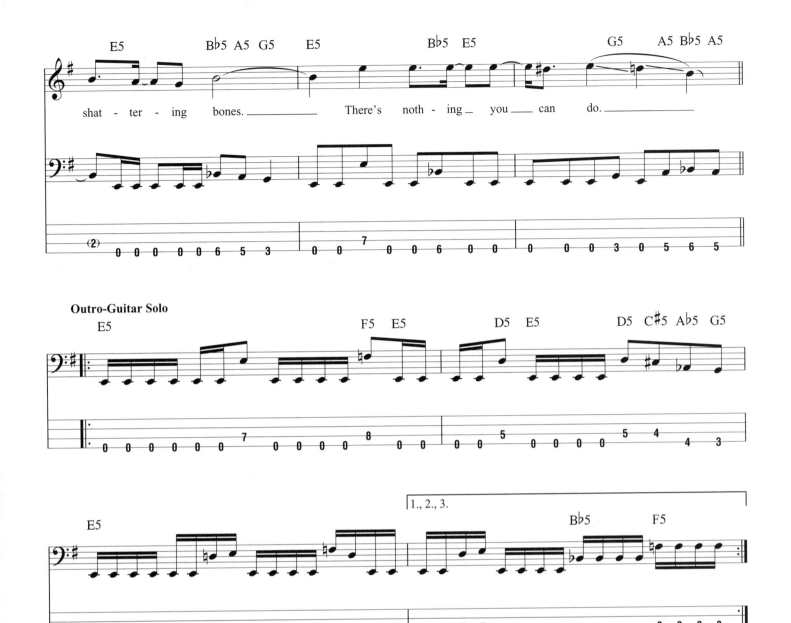

Outro-Guitar Solo

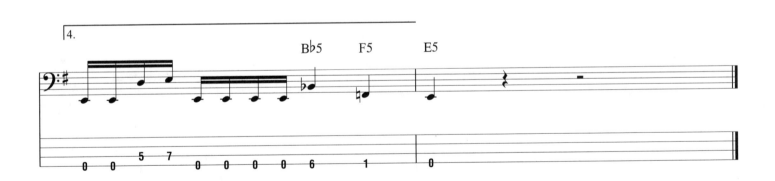

Additional Lyrics

2. The horrific torture device
For those who fail interrogation.
The most painful technique ever known.
People thirst for the worst:
The skull's disintegration.
Beaten, broken, in bloody rags.
Adding insult to injury.
He recants, but it's much too late.
Now let the torture begin!

Holy Wars... The Punishment Due

Words and Music by Dave Mustaine

Intro
Fast ♩ = 164

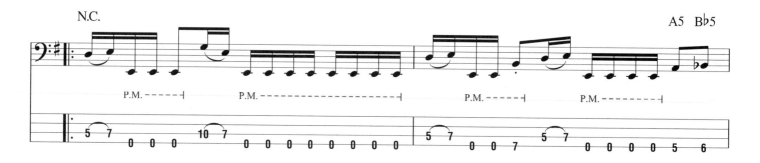

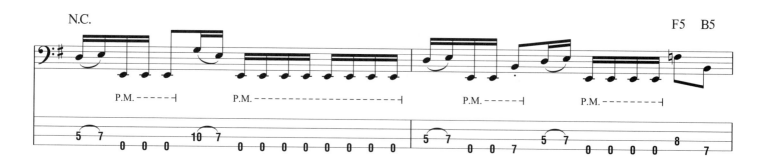

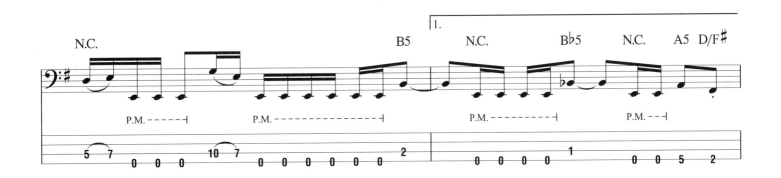

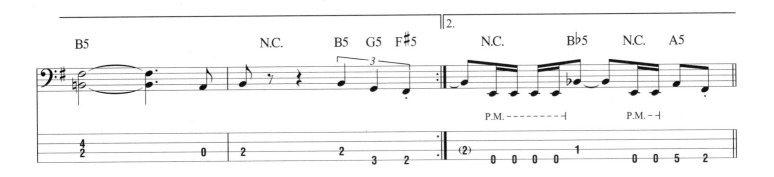

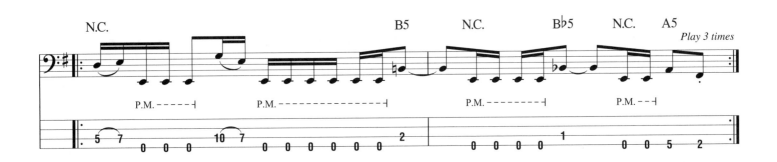

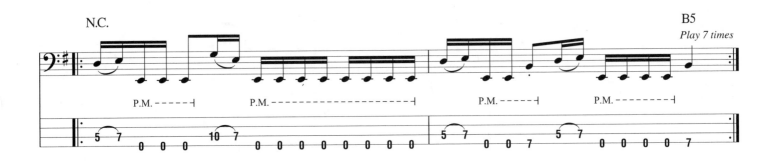

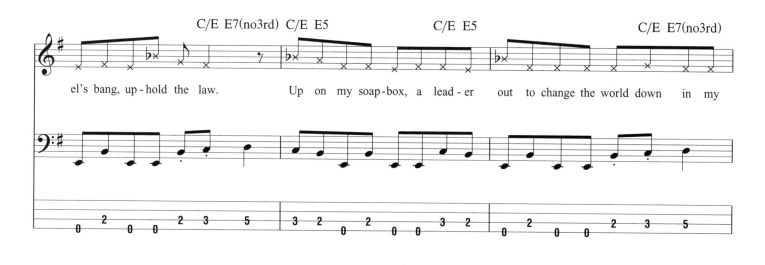

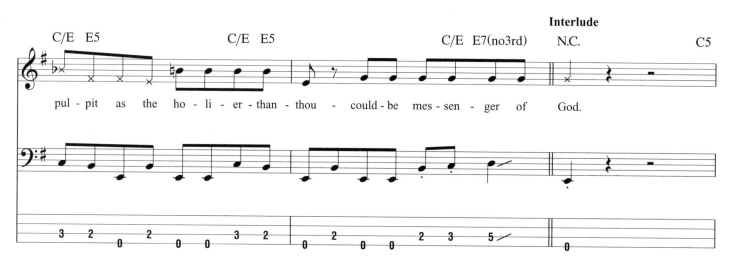

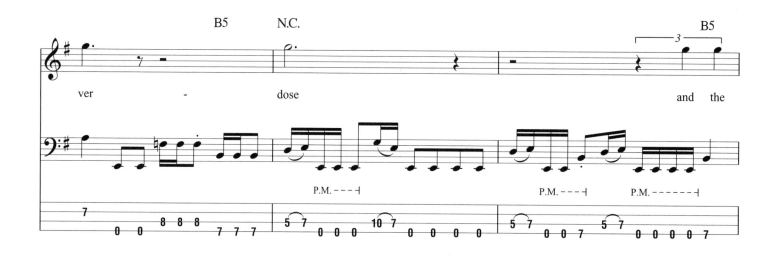

ver - dose

and the

lack

of mer - cy

kill - ings. _____

Mer - cy kill - ings.

Mer - cy

kill - ings,

kill - ings,

Additional Lyrics

2. Fools like me who cross the sea
   And come to foreign lands
   Ask the sheep for their beliefs.
   Do you kill on God's command?

3. A country that's divided
   Surely will not stand.
   My past erased, no more disgrace.
   No foolish naive stand.

4. The end is near, it's crystal clear,
   Part of the master plan.
   Don't look now to Israel.
   It might be your homeland.
   Holy wars.

6. They killed my wife and my baby
   With hopes to enslave me.
   First mistake... last mistake!
   Paid by the alliance to slay all the giants.
   Next mistake... no more mistakes!

Peace Sells

Words and Music by Dave Mustaine

Intro

Moderately fast ♩ = 138

1. What do you mean I don't be - lieve in God? _
2. *See additional lyrics*

Talk to him ev-'ry day.

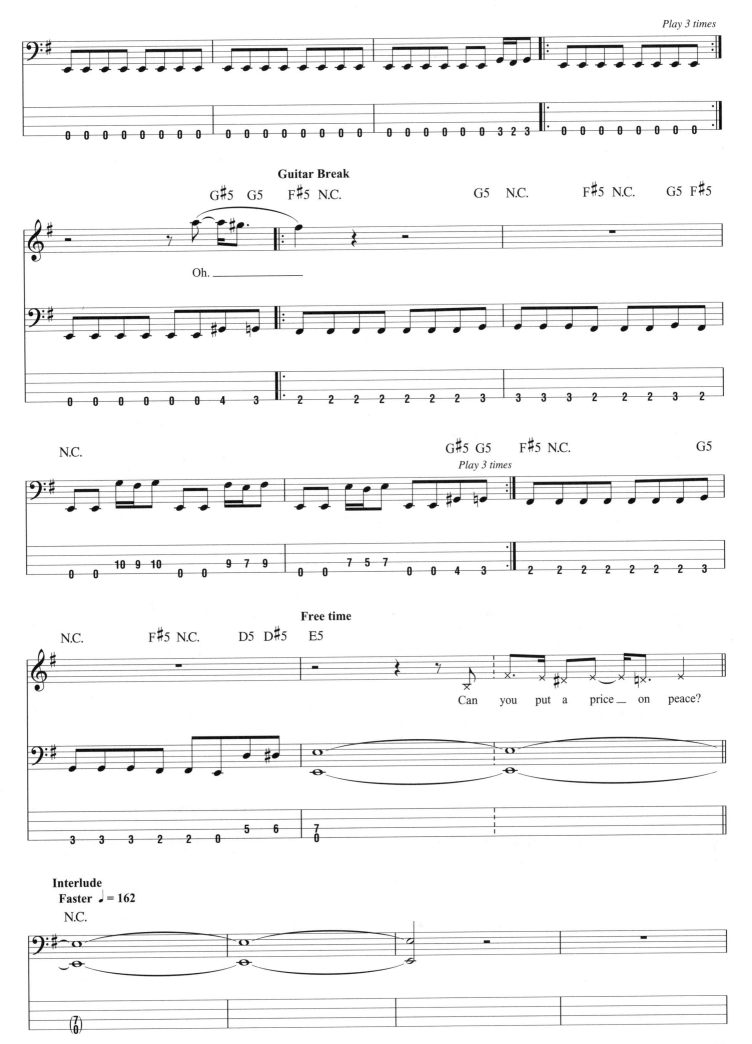

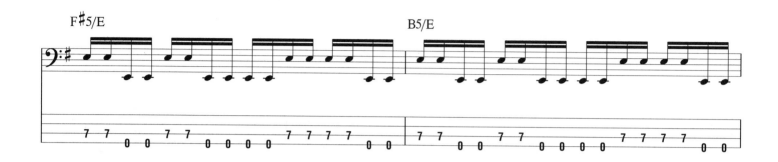

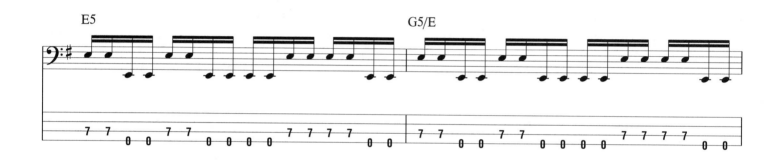

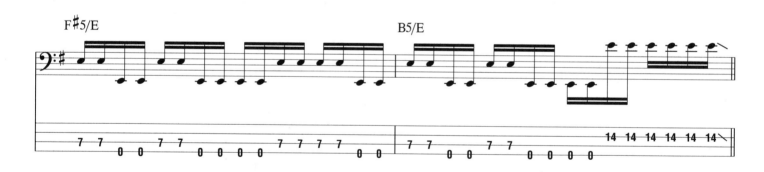

Bridge

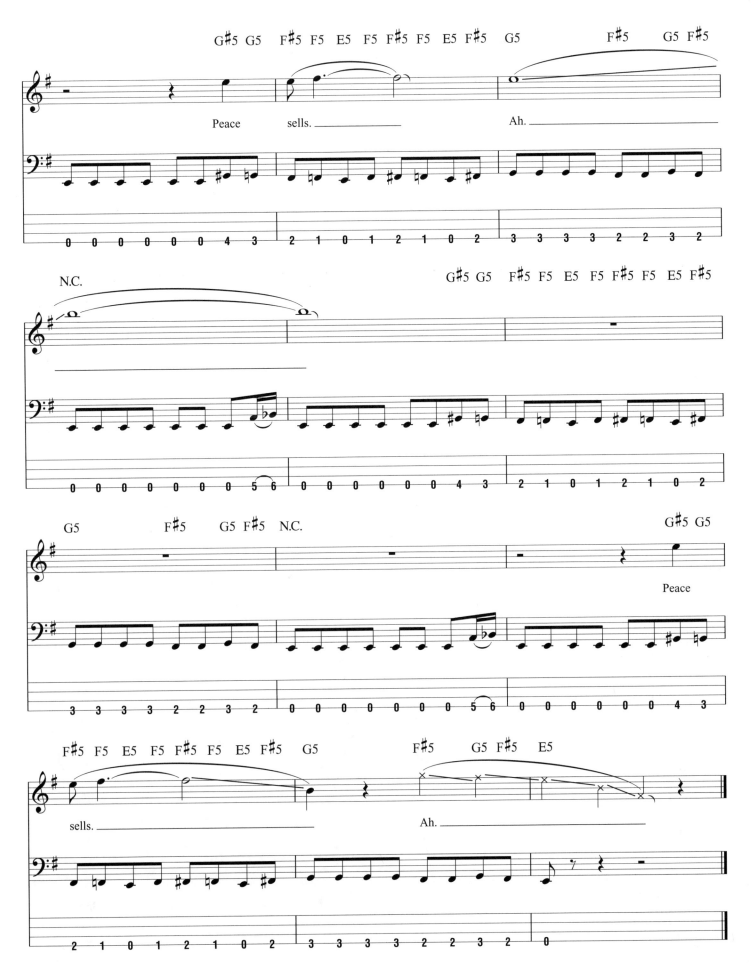

Additional Lyrics

2. What do you mean I hurt your feelings? I didn't know you had any feelings.
   What do you mean I ain't kind? Just not your kind.
   What do you mean I couldn't be the President of the United States of America?
   Tell me something, it's still "We the People," right?

Sweating Bullets

Words and Music by Dave Mustaine

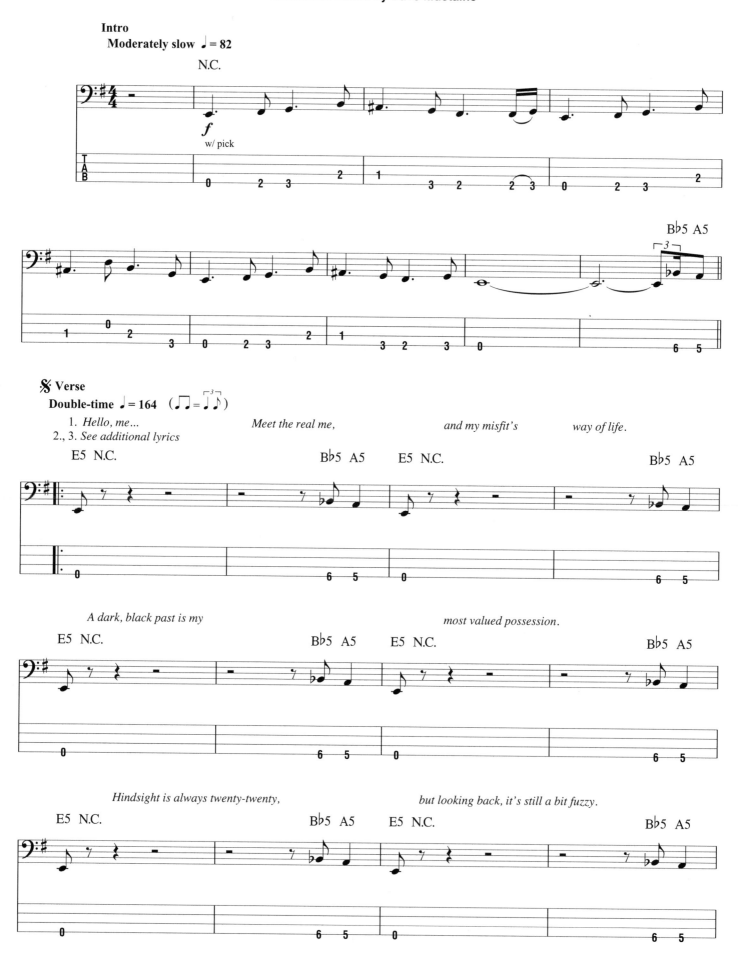

Speak of mutually assured destruction?   *Nice story...*   *Tell it to Reader's Digest.*

Chorus

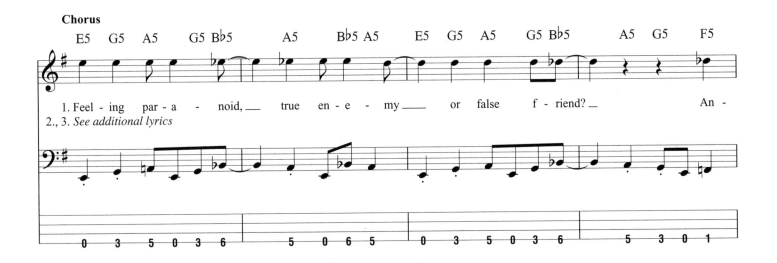

1. Feel - ing par - a - noid, ___ true en - e - my ___ or false f - riend? ___ An -
2., 3. *See additional lyrics*

xi - e - ty's at - tack - ing me ___ and my air is get - ting thin. ___ I'm ___

___ in trou - ble for ___ the things ___ I have - n't got ___ to yet. ___ I'm

Additional Lyrics

2. Hello me... It's me again.
   You can subdue, but never tame me.
   It gives me a migraine headache
   Thinking down to your level.
   Yea, just keep on thinking it's my fault.
   And stay an inch or two outta kicking distance.
   Mankind has got to know
   His limitations.

3. Well me... it's nice talking to myself,
   A credit to dementia.
   Some day you too will know my pain,
   And smile its blacktooth grin.
   If the war inside my head
   Won't take a day off I'll be dead.
   My icy fingers claw your back,
   Here I come again.

Chorus 2. Feeling claustrophobic, like the walls are closing in.
   Blood stains on my hands and I don't know where I've been.
   I'm in trouble for the things I haven't got to yet.
   I'm sharpening the axe and my palms are getting wet,
   Sweating bullets.

Chorus 3. Feeling paranoid, true enemy or false friend?
   Anxiety's attacking me and my air is getting thin.
   Feeling claustrophobic, like the walls are closing in.
   Blood stains on my hands and I don't know where I've been.

Train of Consequences

Words and Music by Dave Mustaine, Dave Ellefson, Nick Menza and Martin Friedman

5-string bass, tune down 1/2 step:
(low to high) Bb-Eb-Ab-Db-Gb

Intro
Moderate Rock ♩ = 114

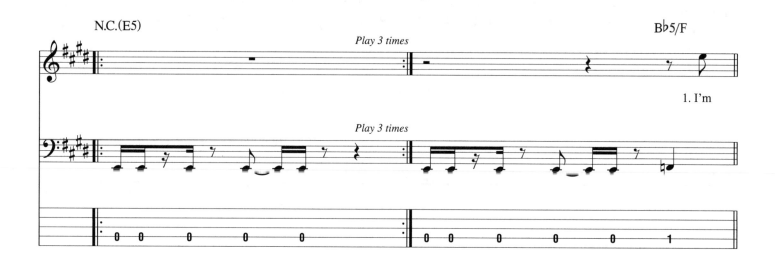

Verse

do-ing you a fa-vor as I'm tak-ing all your mon-ey. I
2. *See additional lyrics*

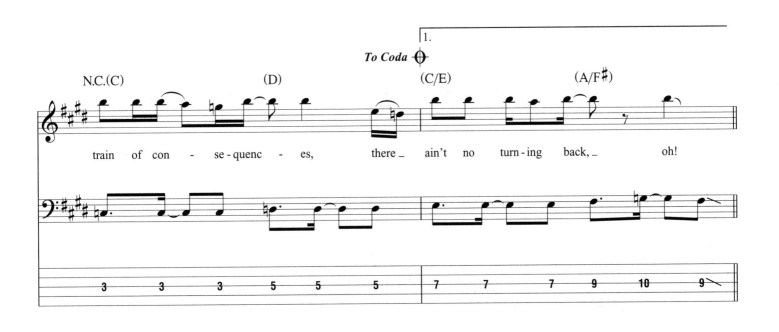

train of con - se - quenc - es, there _ ain't no turn-ing back, _ oh!

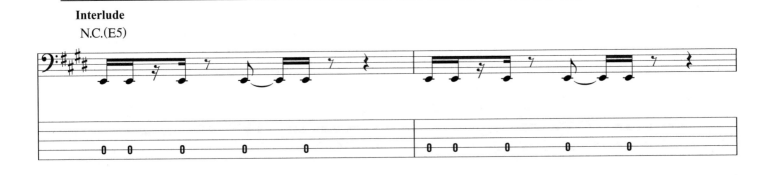

Interlude

N.C.(E5)

Bb5/F

2.

ain't no turn - ing back. __

Interlude

N.C.

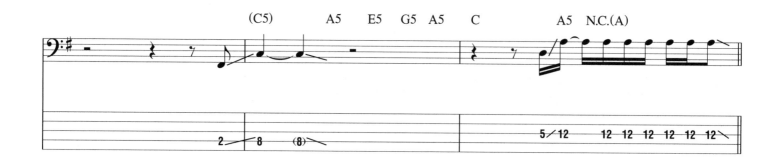

Guitar Solo

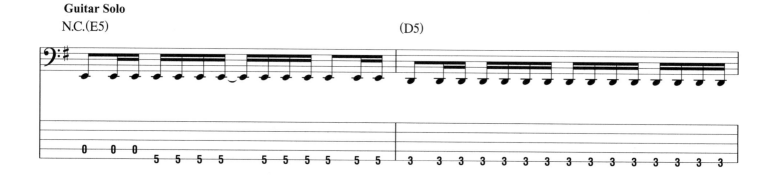

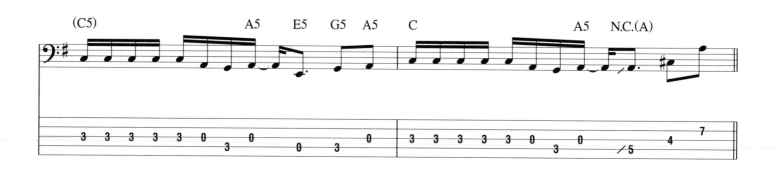

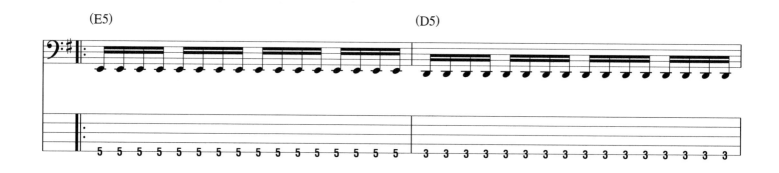

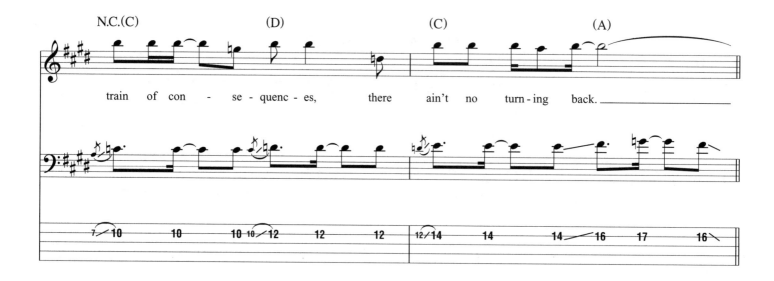

train of con - se - quenc - es, there ain't no turn - ing back. _____

Outro

N.C.(E5)

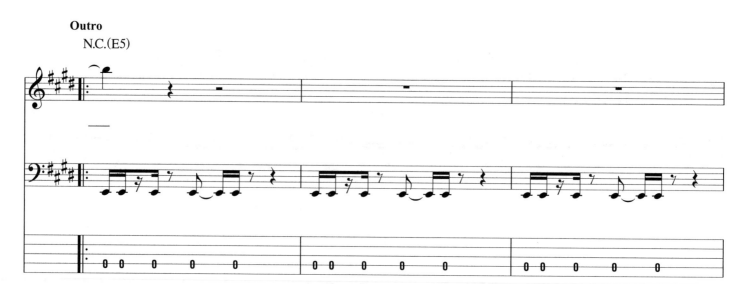

Additional Lyrics

2. No horse ever ran as fast as the money that you bet.
   I'm blowing on my cards, and I play them to my chest.
   Life's fabric is corrupt, shot through with corroded thread.
   As for me, I hocked my brains, packed my bags and headed west, ah.

Pre-Chorus I hocked my brains,
Headed west, oh.

Trust

Words and Music by Dave Mustaine and Marty Friedman

Additional Lyrics

2. Time and again,
   She repeats, "Let's be friends."
   I smile and say yes.
   Another truth bends, I must confess.
   I try to let go,
   But I know we'll never end 'til we're dust.
   We lied to each other again.
   (I wish I could trust.)
   But I wish I could trust.

HAL•LEONARD BASS PLAY-ALONG

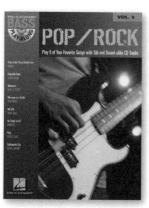

The Bass Play-Along™ Series will help you play your favorite songs quickly and easily! Just follow the tab, listen to the CD to hear how the bass should sound, and then play along using the separate backing tracks. The melody and lyrics are also included in the book in case you want to sing, or to simply help you follow along. The CD is enhanced so you can use your computer to adjust the recording to any tempo without changing pitch!

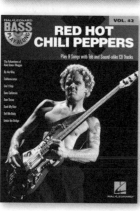

1. Rock
00699674 Book/CD Pack.............$12.95

2. R&B
00699675 Book/CD Pack.............$14.99

3. Pop/Rock
00699677 Book/CD Pack.............$12.95

4. '90s Rock
00699679 Book/CD Pack.............$12.95

5. Funk
00699680 Book/CD Pack.............$12.95

6. Classic Rock
00699678 Book/CD Pack.............$12.95

7. Hard Rock
00699676 Book/CD Pack.............$14.95

9. Blues
00699817 Book/CD Pack.............$14.99

10. Jimi Hendrix Smash Hits
00699815 Book/CD Pack.............$17.99

11. Country
00699818 Book/CD Pack.............$12.95

12. Punk Classics
00699814 Book/CD Pack.............$12.99

13. Lennon & McCartney
00699816 Book/CD Pack.............$14.99

14. Modern Rock
00699821 Book/CD Pack.............$14.99

15. Mainstream Rock
00699822 Book/CD Pack.............$14.99

16. '80s Metal
00699825 Book/CD Pack.............$16.99

17. Pop Metal
00699826 Book/CD Pack.............$14.99

18. Blues Rock
00699828 Book/CD Pack.............$14.99

19. Steely Dan
00700203 Book/CD Pack.............$16.99

20. The Police
00700270 Book/CD Pack.............$14.99

21. Rock Band – Modern Rock
00700705 Book/CD Pack.............$14.95

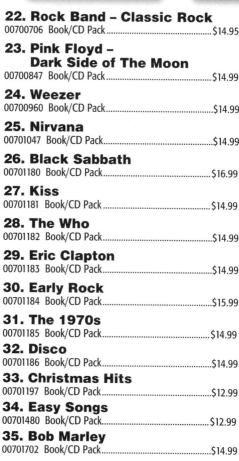

22. Rock Band – Classic Rock
00700706 Book/CD Pack.............$14.95

23. Pink Floyd – Dark Side of The Moon
00700847 Book/CD Pack.............$14.99

24. Weezer
00700960 Book/CD Pack.............$14.99

25. Nirvana
00701047 Book/CD Pack.............$14.99

26. Black Sabbath
00701180 Book/CD Pack.............$16.99

27. Kiss
00701181 Book/CD Pack.............$14.99

28. The Who
00701182 Book/CD Pack.............$14.99

29. Eric Clapton
00701183 Book/CD Pack.............$14.99

30. Early Rock
00701184 Book/CD Pack.............$15.99

31. The 1970s
00701185 Book/CD Pack.............$14.99

32. Disco
00701186 Book/CD Pack.............$14.99

33. Christmas Hits
00701197 Book/CD Pack.............$12.99

34. Easy Songs
00701480 Book/CD Pack.............$12.99

35. Bob Marley
00701702 Book/CD Pack.............$14.99

36. Aerosmith
00701886 Book/CD Pack.............$14.99

37. Modern Worship
00701920 Book/CD Pack.............$12.99

38. Avenged Sevenfold
00702386 Book/CD Pack.............$16.99

40. AC/DC
14041594 Book/CD Pack.............$16.99

41. U2
00702582 Book/CD Pack.............$16.99

42. Red Hot Chili Peppers
00702991 Book/CD Pack.............$19.99

43. Paul McCartney
00703079 Book/CD Pack.............$17.99

44. Megadeth
00703080 Book/CD Pack.............$16.99

45. Slipknot
00703201 Book/CD Pack.............$16.99

49. Eagles
00119936 Book/CD Pack.............$17.99

FOR MORE INFORMATION, SEE YOUR LOCAL MUSIC DEALER, OR WRITE TO:

HAL•LEONARD® CORPORATION
7777 W. BLUEMOUND RD. P.O. BOX 13819 MILWAUKEE, WI 53213

Visit Hal Leonard Online at **www.halleonard.com**
Prices, contents, and availability subject to change without notice.

0414